I0412433

Table of contents

Introduction 1

My story: One of the hardest decision
of my life 4

Habit 1: Responsibility 8

Habit 2: Assume she likes you 13

Habit 3: Do not be afraid of rejection 16

Habit 4: Be a leader 20

Habit 5: Give her a genuine compliment 22

Habit 6: Be funny without being a joke 26

Habit 7: Generate a unique connection
with her 29

Habit 8: Emotional Boundaries 34

Habit 9: Be clear about our life purpose 38

Habit 10: Contact 40

Conclusion 41

Anecdote I: Just Another Night 43

Introduction:

10 simple habits that will increase your dating by 357.14%. Guaranteed!

... Or at least I guarantee that you will not get worse...

Most books or seduction guides will try to give you advice on what to do or say to women. They will tell you which techniques are best for you to get not only her, but any woman and almost instantaneously.

This guide is not about what to say to women, but focuses on creating a more attractive personality. It will not be instantaneous, it will take time, you'll never able conquer them all and many will reject you.

But if I can assure you one thing, it will work!

The reason most books do not work is because they do not address the underlying problem, instead they promote techniques that attempt to compensate for personality deficits. They seek to cover up the problem but not solve it, however your fears and insecurities are still there. **It's like trying to cover the crack in the Titanic with a band aid.** No matter how many you use, it will never be enough.

Those for whom these techniques will be necessary subconsciously feel they are not good enough to conquer them. **Men who are most successful are those who do not see the woman above themselves. Thus the game becomes simple and natural.**

That is why I faithfully believe that success with women is based on the development of our personality. **Self-development and being an attractive man are inseparable.** If you are failing with women, you are doing something wrong. In this guide I will present 10 different habits that will help you do so.

My history ... One of the hardest decisions of my life

"Our future depends on how we understand the past" - Gustavo Cerati (Argentine singer)

My name is Germán Mühlenberg and when I began my studies in seduction and social dynamics in 2008 my situation was very different than it is now.

Like many others who were involved in this subject, I had problems with women. Pursuing any woman who showed a bit of interest in me like a dog with two tails. I was the typical best friend while they were crying for their boyfriends.

My big dream was to find the girl of my dreams with whom I would be happy with the for the rest of my life. I know, I know. I know it sounds like the typical teen chick flick, but that was me.

Although some of them were interested at first, that attraction simply vanished.

I was really lost, had no idea what to do, and also **blamed them**. I considered them silly for being with boys that made them cry instead of me, being a good boy.

It was during a night of frustration that two men on a television program, Martin and Mike, announced that they were starting a seduction academy so I decided to sign up.

It was not easy and I admit it was strange. In addition, it hurt my pride as a "man" to study how to seduce women, something that was supposed to be innate, or at least that was what my parents and society had taught me, I say this, because it was something that was not taught in schools .

But I think the most difficult step was to admit that I had a problem.

That was many years ago and since then, I have become a coach at the same academy and my life has become much more than just finding women. Obviously it was still part of my happiness, but not everything.

Developing myself in an attractive way does not mean for me to say the best lines or to have sex with the greatest number of women. But with a gradual growth of **showing vulnerability, marking emotional boundaries, taking risks and making mistakes. It was not something that happened overnight.**

To be perceived as attractive to a woman is directly proportional to the amount you have invested in, both physically and emotionally, yourself. Self-development and being an attractive man are inseparable. They are the same thing.

Women will be a consequence of a rich and substantial life. **Completely**. That's why I understand that women are not the most important thing in the world, but that they make up only part of it. Women are attracted to men who believe in themselves. Men who know what they want, live life with pride and do not let others dictate it.

I must say, starting to study seduction was one of my most difficult decisions of my life, but also one of the best.

Taking that first step helped to give me much more in different areas of my life.

Habit 1: Responsibility

The first lesson I learned on seduction was that perhaps it wasn't that women were wrong, but that I was wrong in my approach at picking them up. It was ever since then that I started to address the situation differently, and hence obtain different results. A mistake I repeatedly made was giving too much of myself (I tried too hard) to women who didn't reciprocate. I thought that if I showed them I was kind, they would hold me in better regard. Silly me! All I was doing was showing a poor and very needy attitude. How come they ended up with men who didn't value them as I did? Why did they go out with guys who were less attractive than me? I sincerely believed women were very confused. But it was then that I started realizing that it was me who had it all wrong, an insight which put me in an advantageous position. If everything was in the hands of others, then there was nothing I could do to change things. Now, however, I could do something: I could change my attitude and my behavior; and then, women's responses changed. I stopped seeing myself as a victim to women, and gave up trying to seduce them in search of their approval.

I therefore learned that I am responsible for everything that happens in my life: what I accomplish, how I feel, and how others treat me. Instead of pointing fingers and blaming others, I started analyzing my mistakes and looking for ways to do better. It is quite common and normal for our minds to create rationalizations that justify our behavior. This is how we keep pain and rejection at bay, and we keep ourselves clear of any blame, by laying it on others. Through this logic, though, all we accomplish it to always be surrounded by incompetents, when really the change has to come from within. It is important to realize that we are treated however we allow ourselves to be treated. Our behavior affects others' behavior towards us. If women take advantage of us, it's because we let them. If our superiors at work mistreat us, it's because we let them.

The attitude we take towards others will spark a reaction. Whoever thinks women are "cold bitches" should think of what he might be doing to get that response. Those who say that women "are all the same" are most likely putting themselves as victims in order not to take responsibility for their attitude towards others. This is nothing more than a way to dodge responsibility for their mistakes.

This doesn't necessarily mean that those who accuse women are completely mistaken. But even if it were true that, let's say, 50% of women from certain city are immature and malicious, the problem starts when we restrict our focus to that 50%, and place ourselves in the role of victims without looking for any alternatives. We would be allowing those observations to determine the outcome of our attempts. This is just a way to escape the guilt and the sense of responsibility that come from knowing our endeavor was bound to fail.

There are thousands and thousands of single women. If a man cannot find the right woman it is because he is looking in the wrong places. He then judges hundreds of women unfairly because he is not willing to accept the responsibility for his failures. And if you happen to identify with this kind of thinking and attitudes, I recommend you try to become aware of the areas in which you are failing and reflect on that —not just in relation to women, but in your life in general. The world is not against you.

Change the "Why me?" for "What I can do about it?"

Habit 2: Assume she likes you

Stop making excuses to go talk to her and assuming she will not be interested in you because of your own insecurities. Instead, believe that she is interested because you're an interesting person.

Some of the typical excuses:

- *She will not be interested*

- *She is sure to have a boyfriend*

- *She is out of my reach*

- *I should continue reading and practicing*

- *My biceps are not big enough*

This does not mean that sometimes you're not right: Maybe she's not interested, maybe she has a boyfriend or maybe your biceps are not big enough yet. But to assume that she likes you will give you two advantages:

The first is that you are not even allowing yourself to try it when many of those ideas are a figment of your imagination. **She really could be interested in you.**

The second advantage is that you are going to start talking to her with a different attitude. It does not matter if it is talking to a woman, starting a new project or winning a football game. It is proven that having **a positive, realistic attitude** generates more **assertiveness for the achievement of our goals.**

So every time you see a girl you like, say "hello", from me.

I'll take a break here as I do not want to sound like typical uplifting books. To assume that someone likes us in itself is vague and superficial. It would be impossible to achieve this in a real and consistent way if we do not invest in ourselves and have no projects or ambitions.

As I say in Seduction Simplified: "How attractive we are to women is directly proportional to the amount of energy we have invested in ourselves, both physically and emotionally." If we have a strong appreciation for ourselves, it is difficult for us to meet someone whom we believe is not within our reach.

Habit 3: Do not be afraid of rejection

I have met many people who place too much importance on a rejection as if it has a real meaning. The only thing you are avoiding is **learning,** and saving yourself from the discomfort of that "no". She does not know you and there may be thousands of reasons why she does not want to be with you, such as "your biceps are very small"... just kidding.

The truth is that often we judge a **rejection** from our own metrics and insecurities. Sure, she rejected me because I'm ugly, my hair does not look good, I'm a loser, my sneakers are not Nike, etc. All crap.

Their reasons for rejecting you may be very different from those we imagine, so we should care very little because her opinion shouldn't affect our life. If we think that she is right and we don't like something about our condition, we should work to change it or improve it, not victimize our self and cry about it.

I've been years in the field of seduction and received hundreds of rejections, probably many more that anyone who is reading this guide. I admit that some have hurt me, from either inexperience or being attacked unfairly.

I remember one night, having already been some months as a coach, I saw a girl sitting in a disco and I sat next to her. I was aware that it was a risky move but nothing I had not done before.

She looked at me with the face of a rabid dog, almost foaming at the mouth as she barked insults at me. Completely rejected, I left with my tail between my legs and I could not get close to another girl all night. I felt horrible.

I have had very few rejections like that and today they mean nothing to me. She probably had a bad day. Maybe she broke up with her boyfriend or her dog had died. Maybe she didn't like my face but why should I care?

Failures are nothing but experiences and a life full of experiences is a richer life. Whether they are good or bad experiences will always depend on our way of looking at it and what we learn.

When approaching a woman we should always assume that she is attracted to us, although of course, this is not always the case. Most women will not be available or interested in us. However, if we assume that they are it will make it easier to approach them and even to get rejected... I mean, they're the ones missing out anyway.

Never pretend that approaches are perfect. Many times they are disorderly, improvised, unpredictable, clumsy, stupid or ridiculous. Let's embrace randomness and disorder, accept that they will never be perfect and just get close to her!

If she rejects us we can simply move on to the next girl until we find someone who we match up well with. Most people tend to take rejections personally, which is a way to see everything that others say about us as something real.

Do not expect everyone to accept you.

Habit 4: Be a Leader

Leading means taking the first step, most women will wait for you to do it. This does not mean giving orders but giving a direction. Taking risks is part of leadership and means being willing to be rejected. You have to go for the first kiss, turning a conversation sexual, annoying or playing with her or even something as simple as telling her when something does not seem right. If she does it first it is fine, just do not wait for the initiative to come from her.

One tip I think serves well is to change indecisive words like **"maybe"** and replace them with assertive words like **"let's", "I want ..." "We can go to**..." etc. it shows that you have defined ideas and goals.

Even if she rejects you, in many cases she will respect for having balls to have tried.

Habit 5: Give her a genuine compliment

Show her that you like her giving her a genuine compliment. No need to say that at the beginning, but at some point in the conversation. The best way is being clear and specific with the **first thing that catches your attention**. Maybe it's her red lipstick, her tender smile or how much you like her hair pulled back. If you have trouble saying anything specific, just use generic compliment such as "You look incredible."

It is important to note that these compliments are sexual, not emotional. **Expressing our sexual desire** is crucial if you do not want to end up in "The dead zone"... I say "The friend zone". Unless, of course, that is your wish.

The truth is that women want to feel admired and desired. But there is a big difference between **expressing our sexual desire honestly and selflessly** and an **adulation** that is dishonest and looks for a reaction from the other party.

The main problem lies in wanting people to respond in a certain way, and in being needy; as we say in Argentina: using *chamullos*. There is a difference between complimenting someone because of what we think or feel about them, and complimenting someone because we want something from them. It's like buying a girl a drink so that she will be with you, or telling your girlfriend you love her so that she will say it back —that's manipulative. If we really want to say something, because we feel the need to express our feelings, that's perfectly alright. But we shouldn't expect anything in return.

A funny anecdote was when I was in Vietnam and met a girl at my hotel. From the beginning we had an amazing connection and we talked for half an hour without stopping sharing our experiences. Actually, everything was fine but at no time had I shown sexual interest with her.

Now what I did after I cannot say if was right or wrong, it just came to mind. "*The truth is you're a very sexy girl*" I said without any holding back. Her eyes widened as if not believing what I had just said. My feeling was that she had not liked it and she disappeared. I just went on with my life.

The next day we met again, had an incredible afternoon, kissed and lived happily ever after... okay, at least until our trip separated us.

A few days later, I asked her what she had thought about my straight forward comment about how attractive she looked. She told me she had been very surprised and had not known how to react.

I confessed I was afraid that she would see me as a friend after our nice talk. She laughed and said that before I said that she thought I was just being friendly.

Women want to be desired, and the more assertive we are in demonstrating our desire, the stronger their excitement will be, even when they have initially showed no interest. Status itself attracts women as it makes them see us as a potential partner. Being physically assertive and sexually direct triggers a woman's sexual arousal.

Remember, if she really interests you - tell her, because even if you fail, you make clear what your intentions are, and you show that you have the courage to say it.

Habit 6: Be funny without being a joke

It is well known that laughter is one of the classic tools in seduction. By definition, flirting is a way of expressing our sexuality in a manner that women will find attractive without looking needy, which is always a plus in terms of attraction. The most frequently used flirting techniques are joking around or making fun of the other person. We can hardly attract a girl if we do not make her laugh.

But flirting is not everything in itself: you may be the funniest guy of the group, or the one with the best magic tricks, but if you don't advance sexually. You will inevitably end up falling into the friend zone.

In his book *Double your Dating*, writer David DeAngelo suggests a number of amusing attitudes that can be employed when flirting:

- **Misinterpreting what women say**: For instance, if she says "*Let's do it*" (no matter the context), we could answer, "*Hey, I think you are going too fast.*"
- **Fishing for sexual innuendo:** If she says she is cold, we could tell her, *"You are not getting a hug from me."* If she says she's hot, we could remark, "*It's just that you are standing too close to me.*" If she asks, *"How long?"* we could say something like, "*Shall I get something to measure it?*"
- **Exaggerating what she says or does:** We could resort to lines like, *"This purse is huge! Are you carrying a gun?",* or, if she were holding a green drink, *"That looks radioactive."* If she said something like *"I'm having a bad hair day",* we could observe *"I didn't want to say*

anything, but now that you mention it…" (take care not to cross the line when it comes to matters of looks or age —if she says she says she's fat, avoid telling her she looks like a whale).

- **Making funny associations:** Try to connect the situation you are in with elements from popular culture, whether it be TV programmes, movies, books, etc.

It is important not to be excessive, not to be trying to maintain the interaction, but something that is natural. In humor, it always works well to maintain a serious posture when we make a joke and not be the first to laugh.

Remember that the phrases themselves mean nothing, but it is the attitude and behavior that express value.

Habit 7: Generate a unique connection with her

A unique connection is the basis for any relationship: family, friends and couple. These make us subconsciously feel we always knew that person which generates confidence.

We all have jokes that only our best friends understand and no one else knows what the hell we are laughing at. The internal jokes are related to specific places, or the experience of shared moments, which make a person generate happy memories with us. The more happy memories she has with us, the more important we will be in her life.

Some EXAMPLES creating a unique connection:

- *You can annoy her with something she has said incorrectly and create a funny nickname about it.*

- *Expressing our opinions honestly and not taking it back if she disagrees with our values, this is important to make real and authentic connections.*

Generating a unique connection is intimately linked to being vulnerable. It is simply to show ourselves as we are, that is as someone who does not pretend to be perfect.

During my years as a coach, in which I advised hundreds of men, the trait I found they all had in common was the inability to express their emotions freely. In fact, this is a problem I also used to have. If we try to conceal ourselves and pretend we are something we are not, then we will find ourselves torn by a great incongruity. In contrast, if we open up and show ourselves as we really are, with our strengths and weaknesses, we will be proving that we are not afraid of exposing ourselves, that we are not afraid of rejection. Strong people can open up without fearing getting hurt. They generally put their own beliefs and values before those of others, unless they decide it best to do otherwise. These people are willing to run risks.

Exposing ourselves puts us in an attractive light. If someone is able to expose their weaknesses, it is because they are strong, not weak. Certain actions which are in most cases interpreted as signs of weakness, actually take a lot of courage, like telling someone how much they move us or how happy their presence makes us. These situations expose us to rejection, but this is not a bad thing, I would even dare say it is a good thing. It's as the saying goes: "what doesn't kill you makes you stronger".

Being exposed to rejection can strengthen our belief in ourselves. It may also make us feel uncomfortable, I'm not saying it won't, but it is that very feeling which will make us stronger. But we must be clear about what the intention is. If our intention is to impress someone, we are not really exposing ourselves. There is no real connection to our emotions and that is what really matters. The exhibition does not have to do directly with what we say but with the emotions we want to convey. And it is in sharing the same emotions where the connection with the other person is generated. Understand this: here it is not possible to cheat! We can simulate having the same emotion, but I would not recommend it. It doesn't work in the long run or make you a better person.

If you are not doing well with women, you are probably having trouble expressing your true emotions and intentions, and getting in touch with your feelings. Perhaps conversations with women end up becoming dull because you try to avoid saying things which might upset them. Or because you delay kissing them out of fear of being rejected. Or because you don't want to do anything which might make them uncomfortable. All these issues have a common origin: the inability to express ourselves freely.

It is necessary to speak of feelings. If we try to expose ourselves with a girl just to go to bed with her, the only thing we are going to end up doing is exposing our desire to end up in her bed. We must be honest with our intentions. It is important to be authentic, even when you are afraid or nervous to show yourself in such a way.

Habit 8: Emotional boundaries

Those people with well-defined emotional boundaries are responsible for their emotions and actions. They determine a healthy, strong identity and not a needy one. They do not play the victim or blame others for what happens to them.

Most fights between couples usually occur because they do not establish the emotional boundaries that correspond to each party well. On the contrary, if each of the members of a couple assumes their own emotional responsibility, they will achieve a healthy relationship.

The relationships that work best are those in which you do not need to blame your partner for your emotional state. An example of this could be if your girlfriend forbids you from seeing your friends because it creates jealousy. If you are not giving real reasons for that to happen she should be responsible for how she feels, it is product of her insecurity (unless of course, you are being unfaithful).

On the other hand, if you let her interfere and you do not see your friends you are showing weak emotional boundaries that also show great insecurity.

Forms of not respecting the boundaries

- *Does not respect when you say "no" or "yes" / Does not know how to say "yes" or "no"*
- *Does not respect your physical space / Does not respect her physical space*

- *Does not respect you physically or emotionally / Does not respect others physically or emotionally*

- *Someone who always wants to be right / You always want to be right*

- *Someone who never keeps their promises / You never keep your promises*

- *Being attacked, whether with jokes or not, periodically / That attacks others*

- *That they tell you what you need or what you should feel / That you tell others what they need or should feel*

- *That invalidates your feelings by dictating what you should feel / That invalidates the feelings of others*

Personal boundaries are determined by how responsible you are for your own emotions and actions, as well as not taking responsibility for the emotions and actions of others.

A relationship should not be determined by demands and sacrifices whether with your partner, friends or family. This does not mean that sometimes we do things for others for the simple reason of wanting to. **The problem lies with waiting for something in return or being afraid of the consequences if we do not.**

Habit 9: Be clear about our life purpose

The purpose of life is to follow our own passion. Make your life an adventure that they want to be part of. I talk more about this topic in "**Happiness Simplified.**" This is a point that perhaps many fail on, and it is very common to see how there are relationships that decay by the simple fact that men put them as a higher priority, thus losing their own identity.

There are those who leave all their activities or friends for their partner. **They make them the center of their universe, which is very unattractive.** No matter how virtuous it may be, it will inevitably be a relationship with an expiration date.

Lack of self-confidence and lack of a clear purpose for life are the main

shortcomings of an emotionally helpless person, who will tend to prioritize others rather than themselves.

Do not misunderstand me, **it is true that it is important to have a balanced life**, but whatever your life purpose (whether: building a business, studying, traveling the world, etc.), you must give it a certain priority.

Habit 10: Contact

How to get their contact information? Simple, just ask her.

Some examples:

- ○ *I want your number*

- ○ *Give me your facebook*

- ○ *Email?*

Why so simple?

Any woman who is interested in you, will want to give you their contact information, if not, **the problem lay not in how you asked but how the interaction unfolded.**

Go ahead and ask!

Conclusion

Before you go out and use this guide in search of women, there is something else that is important to mention.

Neither this guide nor any book will be the solution to all your problems, but they are tools that together with your commitment can take you further. As we talked about, the development and investment in our person is very important to generate attraction in women, but even more important for our relationships and happiness.

The idea is not to create a life that revolves around women but that they are the ones that want to fit yours. An attractive personality does not consist of phrases or lines but a certain character of its own.

As you get to grips with these issues, your confidence will gradually grow. **That is why it is important that you take action and put into practice everything you just read to incorporate and naturalize these habits.**

Anecdote I: Just Another Night

It was a Friday night in Montpellier, France. I found myself quite tired after working all week. I was indecisive about whether or not to go out for the night because I was scheduled to work again already the next morning at 6 A.M. I decided to do it: "Two short hours, and I'll leave," I told myself.

I had a drink with some of my French friends, but they ultimately decided not to come out, so I set out alone. I arrived and made a quick reconnaissance of the establishment. I was on the third floor when I saw her. I liked her instantly. Dark brown hair, petite, fantastic breasts and well-dressed. She was sitting against the wall and seemed bored and alone. Next to her sat another girl, who was also attractive in a different way, and who seemed to be accompanied by another man. I sat down on her other side, and without an ounce of shyness, extended my hand and introduced myself by name. Surprised, she smiled at me.

The club was dimly lit and the music pounded. I began to talk to her in my basic, strongly-accented English while memorizing the details of her face. I always do that. Up-close, I liked her features even more. Communication was difficult. She told me she was German and had the accent to confirm it. Her name was Julieane.

I noticed an acceleration in her speech, as if she were a bit nervous. She was also struggling to understand what I was saying. Her dominion of the English language humiliated mine, I felt like a "brute," but I knew that this also generated a certain charm.

Languages never felt like a barrier for me when it came to communicating with women. At times, I had met girls who used my low language proficiency as an excuse to reject me, but I knew that the real problem wasn't a lack of communication but a lack of interest.

When one person likes another, they'll listen attentively and try to understand regardless of how good or bad the level of the language (unless it's non-existent). In the first few months, I went out to parties and approached girls saying "You like me", when in reality I wanted to tell them "I like you". But truthfully, it didn't make a difference. They already understood my intentions.

We continued to struggle to converse in broken English. I interrupted her with a kiss. She wrapped her arms around me and I did the same, in response. She kissed like an angel, and our kiss lasted several minutes. When we finally stopped, and resumed talking, we were both more relaxed.

Then she introduced me to her companion, who turned out to be French, and as I habitually do, I congratulated the French girl on having such an amazing friend (Juliana). The French girl left us alone, and for a while we took advantage of the time to talk and kiss.

It wasn't long before we left, hand-in-hand, complicit in what we were about to do. We took a taxi to her house. She led me through the doors like a guest of honor. Her flat was lovely, very organized and clean.

Now there wasn't any loud music or dim light. We started in the kitchen. In some ways, we looked at each other as two strangers who were seeing each other for the first time. We spoke a bit. My brain collected new information about her and I began to perceive her more as a woman and less as just a girl in a bar.

She was delicate, somewhat structured but at the same time, sensitive and simple. She had deep brown eyes and blinked up at me when she was trying to understand what I was saying. She offered me a glass of wine, but I asked for a glass of water instead. This disconcerted her, and for a moment she was quiet, as if it wasn't the response she expected. Then she got two glasses.

We went to her room. She had an ample bed with a large window behind it. A desk with a computer on it stood to one side with various pieces of furniture surrounding it. I sat on her bed and began to take off my socks. She moved about the room, rearranging things here and there, although it was already quite tidy. Then she returns to me, and after a brief exchange of words, we kissed again. Both of our clothes fell off. Her tits were incredible. I loved this moment; I loved being with her.

We were in her bed, limbs entangled and completely naked. We spoke for a time more, I adored hearing her laugh. Then we fell asleep for a couple hours. I awoke at 4:30am to leave for work. She got up with me and put on her pyjamas. She sweetly opened the door for me and left me with a kiss as if I were her lover leaving for war.

I exited hurriedly, straightening my recently-put-on clothes. I had no idea where I was or how to get to work. Somewhat disoriented, I began searching for a taxi. The streets were vacant. As time passed, I started to despair. I broke into a run as I watched my location on my phone, beginning to convince myself that

I wasn't too far, that just maybe I could make it if I ran. I crossed green and wooded landscapes, but I couldn't stop to look at my surroundings. I ran. I ran as fast as I could. I felt short on time and a little desperate. The problem is I'm a very punctual man.

It was 5:57am when I finally arrived and was greeted by a friend. "How are you?" He asked me. I was breathless, starving and sleep-deprived. "Great!" I responded, smiling ear-to-ear.